MW00946154

Finance

A learning workbook program for junior high and high school students.

ISBN-13: 978-1725514713
ISBN-10: 1725514710

Printed by CreateSpace, an Amazon.com company.
Available from Amazon.com and other retail outlets.
CreateSpace, Charleston, SC

Consult a professional when seeking business advice and decisions. This is a learning book discussin
topics in a general style, not intended to be considered professional advice, suggestions, or guidance.

Submit all inquiries at the website www.YMBAgroup.com

Y.M.B.A. Finance - grades 6 7 8 9 10 +   ages 12 13 14 15 16 +

Finance

We hope to hear from you!

We value your suggestions.

Positive feedback, shares and word of mouth appreciated.

Suggestions, Comments, Questions

always welcome at

www.YMBAgroup.com

THE Y.M.B.A. GROUP - FINANCE
Finance, Money and Banking

TABLE OF CONTENTS

We hope to hear from you!

Do you have a suggestion for a book topic?

Let us know and we will consider creating it!

www.YMBAgroup.com

How To Use This Book

Thank you for choosing the Y.M.B.A. learning workbook series. I am excited to share the topics with you. As a teacher, corporate professional, M.B.A. and parent, I sought to find a quality program for my children that was both at an introductory level and interesting for their age. When I discovered nothing like this existed, Y.M.B.A. began. A business learning program for young students created and designed by an M.B.A, teacher, and parent. Y.M.B.A. presents information in clear, easy to follow style; focused on students approximately 12 to 16 years of age. I designed the lessons as a combination textbook and workbook because students retain far more when applying the newly taught ideas. The series instructs one idea at a time in a straightforward and simple to understand format. While presenting students with a concept they develop their understanding with fun, level-appropriate examples. After each lesson page is a worksheet to apply the idea from the page prior. This pattern keeps students engaged and actively learning with on-going student applications. The "The Drawing Board" worksheets reinforce the lesson as students practice reasoning, computation, or analysis. Y.M.B.A. focuses on useful business and everyday topics found across industries and in daily life.

Each learning workbook has a quiz for a student demonstration of their new understanding of the subject. As the student completes the learning workbook you will likely see an increase in both pride and confidence. Why wait for business concepts to be introduced? Students are ready to learn about practical life and business topics today. Y.M.B.A. lessons include relevant examples based on familiar student scenarios to sustain learning that is both effective and fun!

Business skills are useful in every industry; an understanding of business is essential. Why wait? Students can begin achieving more with Y.M.B.A. today and build a path for the future. Your support is appreciated. Suggestions, questions, or comments are always welcome.

Thank you,

L.J. Keller

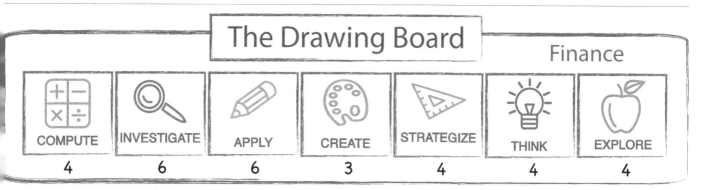

The Drawing Board

Finance

COMPUTE	INVESTIGATE	APPLY	CREATE	STRATEGIZE	THINK	EXPLORE
4	6	6	3	4	4	4

The quantity of each skill practice area is shown below each learning tile.
Worksheet pages seek to capture student interest and build learning momentum.

         www.YMBAgroup.com

What Is Finance?

Finance involves the increase, decrease, and movement of money either within a business, by the government, or as part of personal spending.

How does someone save money for college?

How does a company invest in new equipment?

How can one company buy another company?

All of these questions are answered with finance.

Are You Ready?

How Can Finance Help?

Let's Get Started!

Success is wonderful and congratulations in advance for all you will accomplish!
As you achieve milestones you will have the opportunity to make decisions that build your future. In high school perhaps you will have a job, consider:

What will you choose to do with your earnings?

How will you choose a bank if you borrow money to pay for college tuition?

Which job offer has an overall better salary and benefits package?

Finance has the answer for all of these questions.

By the end of this workbook you will be able to write a check, use a check register, consider different investment options, appreciate the value of savings, read a credit report, understand corporate stock and discuss risk and investments.
Note, information in this workbook should not be considered investment suggestions.
If you choose to invest, be sure to research and discuss based on your personal goals.

A *prospectus* is a document prepared by a company to share the details of the business. The goal is to show an investor that an investment in the business is a good decision.

Jobs In Finance and Banking

Bank Teller	Account Auditor	Prospectus Writer
Mortgage Banker	Chief Financial Officer (CFO)	Bond Advisor
Investment Director	Mutual Fund Account Manager	Stock Broker

The Drawing Board

Match the term with the word it is describing. If you are unsure of a word use a dictionary to find the meaning. Draw a line to the definition in the next column.

asset

Person who gives money in the hope that the company will return the amount, plus extra money called interest.

stock

A company sales less expenses equals the money the company made in the business.

investor

Company 1 and company 2 come together and may create new company 3.

merger

An item of value that is owned and is cash or may be sold for cash.

interest rate

The amount of money earned on an investment usually paid monthly or annually.

acquisition

Purchased by shareholders who want to own a part of the corporation.

return

Company 1 takes over company 2 and only company 1 continues to exist.

profit

The amount of money an investment returns to an investor, a percent.

earnings

The money earned by an investor after expenses and fees are deducted.

EXPLORE

www.YMBAgroup.com

Have you ever wondered how people were able to acquire
new items before coins and cash were invented?

Long ago, beads were used as a method of trade to allow people to trade items of similar value. Beads were also helpful when two people wanted to trade two things that were not similar in value. An example would be when one person was looking to trade three chickens for a cow, but the cow owner believed the cow was worth five chickens. In this scenario, the trade would be to barter three chickens, plus ten blue beads, in exchange for one cow.

A popular trade item in the 1700s was the skin of a deer. Deerskin was used for clothes and shelter. A deer was also called a *buck*, the skin was known as "one buckskin. The value during early trade for a buckskin would be known today as one dollar. *Did you know this term is still used today? A dollar bill today is called a buck.*

The amount of trade increased as the population increased. People began moving further and further away from big cities. As this happened the distance to travel to trade increased as well. Traveling with large quantities of items to trade became difficult. The system of payment changed from barter, buckskins and beads to coins and dollar bills. Now people could carry a small bag to have money to trade in place of the larger and heavier trade goods.

As years went by the dollar became the preferred way to acquire goods and services. Banks began to offer people a place to hold and save their money. For more costly items banks started to offer loans. With a loan from the bank the buyer could buy a piece of land and repay the bank a small amount at a time until the full amount is paid. Soon banks realized there were some purchases too costly to pay for with cash, but also too low in price for a bank loan. To meet this need banks began to offer selected customers a credit card. A credit card would allow a buyer to purchase an item when wanted and pay the bank back over time.

The Drawing Board

Barter System Conversions   TOOLBOX

1 Red Bead = 2 Brown Beads   2 Goats = 1 Cow
2 Brown Beads = 1 Chicken   2 Cows = 1 Horse
3 Chickens = 1 Goat   4 Horses = 1 Wagon

1 Red Bead = $2.50   2 Brown Beads = $5

Based On the Information Above: The cost in dollars and cents for each item.

1 Red Bead equals 2 Brown Beads = $5.00 | 2 Goats is $60.00 = 1 Cow
2 Brown Beads is $10.00 = 1 Chicken | 2 Cows is $120 = 1 Horse
3 Chickens is $30.00 = 1 Goat | 4 Horses are $480 = 1 Wagon

Look at the items picked up on a trip to the market 200 years ago.
Write the total spent on the trip on the line next to each list.

1. $ _____

6 chickens
2 cows
1 goat

4. $ _____

1 chicken
1 horse

2. $ _____

2 horses
1 wagon

5. $ _____

8 goats
2 wagons

3. $ _____

4 cows
8 chickens

6. $ _____

1 cow
1 goat
1 wagon

COMPUTE

         www.YMBAgroup.com

How Does Money Have Value?

Did you know .... If the date was February 15, 1970 you could take your cash paper money to specific government locations and trade it for gold or silver. The ability to trade money for gold or silver was because the paper money was guaranteed (backed) by the government. The government told users of the currency that they had an equal value in gold and silver to support the value of the money. Without gold and silver money was just paper. Then in 1971, the United States approved a plan that stated the government would no longer accept cash trades for gold and silver. The United States of America was going to change to a system that used *fiat money*. Buyers and sellers would now decide the value of the money.

Fiat Money is a system of currency (money) where the value of the money is determined by supply and demand. The money itself has no value. The value comes from how much demand people have for the money. More demand creates more valuable money. Less demand makes money less valuable.

Fiat money gets its value from how many people want the money.
More demand makes the money more valuable. If a government prints money to add it to the economy there will be a lot of money that was not demanded.
More printed money will make it easier to get money.
If it is easier to get money then there will be less demand.
Less demand will make the value of the money go down.
Therefore, adding money to the marketplace causes money to have less value.

12

Future demand can be reliably predicted in a stable market since the population grows at a predictable rate. The consistent amount of demand is because the population of a country or marketplace grows at a steady anual rate.

Plot the annual population of Diversifyatopia on the graph below. The first item of data has been completed as shown by the star.

(1977, 1 million)   (1992, 2.5 million)
(1982, 1.5 million)   (1997, 3 million)
(1987, 2 million)   (2002, 3.5 million)

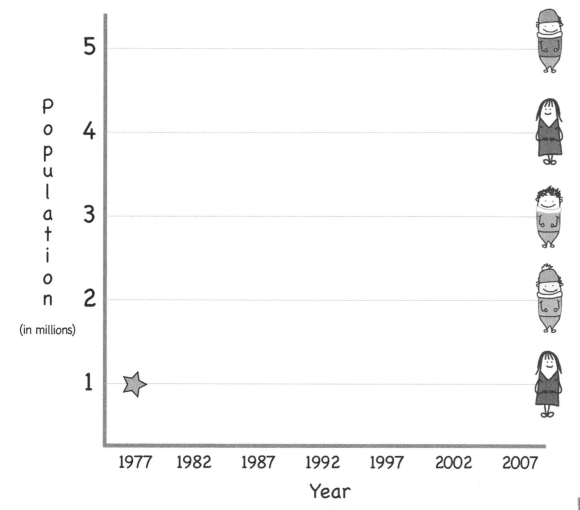

1. Based on the data and the graph, what do you think the population of Diversifyatopia was in the year 2007? _____ million people.

INVESTIGATE

www.YMBAgroup.com

The F.D.I.C. - Federal Deposit Insurance Corporation

The F.D.I.C. is a corporation in the United States of America that was created by Congress. The goal of the F.D.I.C. is to give people confidence that if they deposit their money in a bank that the bank will return it to them when they want to make a withdrawal. Why would the government want people *to save* their money in banks? When a person deposits money in the bank, the bank is then able to loan the money to customers requesting a loan from the bank. A loan makes it possible for a purchase to happen. Purchases keep the marketplace busy with buyers and sellers. A busy marketplace creates a need for employees.

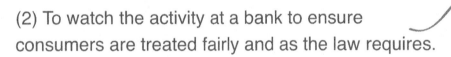

There are three key goals of the F.D.I.C.:

(1) To provide insurance to bank customers who deposit at a bank. If a bank does not have the money to give a customer at the time of a requested withdrawal the F.D.I.C. will make the money available so the customer can withdraw their funds.

Federal Deposit Insurance Corporation

(2) To watch the activity at a bank to ensure consumers are treated fairly and as the law requires.

(3) If a bank decides to no longer be in business the F.D.I.C. will assist the bank in closing. This will help customers ensure their money and investments are returned.

The F.D.I.C. is managed by five people who are selected by a president and approved by Congress.

The idea for the F.D.I.C. came after the 1920's financial troubles and the stock market crash of 192? in the United States that caused many banks to close.

The F.D.I.C. is based in Washington, D.C., with additional locations across the United States.

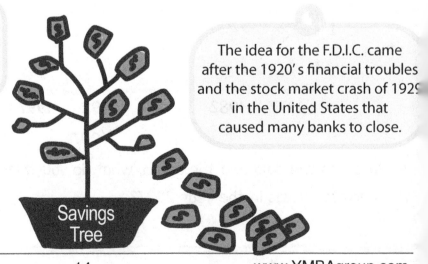

Savings Tree

The Drawing Board

Select the best answer for the true and false questions below. If you select false, circle the word that is not correct, then write the word that would more correctly belong in the sentence.

1. Increasing the number of shoppers and sellers creates a need for fewer jobs.

     True   False, the correct word is _____

2. The goal of the F.D.I.C. is to ensure pencils are available to bank customers.

     True   False, the correct word is _____

3. The F.D.I.C. headquarters is located in Albany, New York.

     True   False, the correct word is _____

4. The abbreviation F.D.I.C. stands for Fun Deposit Insurance Corporation.

     True   False, the correct word is _____

5. The government doesn't want people to save money in a bank.

     True   False, the correct word is _____

6. A bank uses diamonds deposited from customers to loan to other customers.

     True   False, the correct word is _____

7. One goal of the F.D.I.C. is to make envelopes available to banks.

     True   False, the correct word is _____

8. A second goal of the F.D.I.C. is to assist the bank in painting.

     True   False, the correct word is _____

9. The F.D.I.C. is managed by eight people who are approved by Congress.

     True   False, the correct word is _____

10. The idea for the F.D.I.C. came after the financial troubles in the 1970s.

     True   False, the correct word is _____

STRATEGIZE

Congratulations! You just opened your first checking account at a bank.

The bank provides a checkbook and a check register along with a welcome note

to thank you for choosing to invest your money at their location.

But how do you write a check?

Did you know that writing a check is the same process each time. The parts that are completed to make a payment include the date, who is being paid, where the payment should be applied, how much is being spent and the signature of the person making the payment.

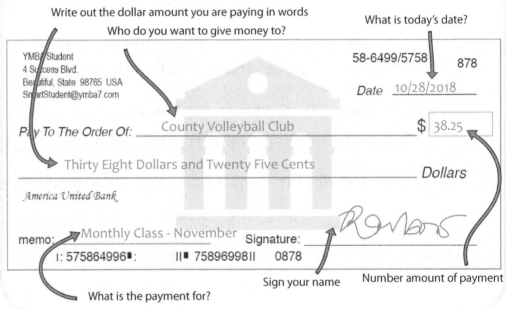

Write out the dollar amount you are paying in words
Who do you want to give money to?
What is today's date?

YMBA Student
4 Success Blvd.
Beautiful, State 98765 USA
SmartStudent@ymba7.com

58-6499/5758   878

Date 10/28/2018

Pay To The Order Of: _____ County Volleyball Club _____ $ 38.25

_____ Thirty Eight Dollars and Twenty Five Cents _____   Dollars

America United Bank

memo: ___ Monthly Class - November ___   Signature: _____

I: 575864996■:   II■ 7589699811   0878

What is the payment for?

Sign your name   Number amount of payment

1. Date check is written.
2. Payee: Person or Business that receives the check.
3. Amount of check written in numbers.
4. Amount of check written in words.
5. The account number or reason for payment.
6. Payor: Person or Business that writes the check.

Check Writing Terms:

Check Register: A book to keep a record of all your bank transactions.

Check Endorsement: Written on the back of a check to deposit the check.

Minimum Balance: The minimum amount of money required in your account.

Service Charge: Possible bank charges (fees) for having or using the account.

Non-Sufficient Funds: (NSF) Not payable, not enough money in the bank account.

Complete the check numbers 873 to 875 for each of the scenarios presented on the stub next to each check. You may look at the previous page for details and instructions about how to correctly fill in the information on a check.

Check Stub	Checks To Write

Check Stub

Date
October 7, 2018

Company
Clong Electric

Amount
$64.31

Memo
September
Electric

YMBA Student
4 Success Blvd.
Beautiful, State 98765 USA
info@ymbagroup.com

58-6499/5758   873

Date _____

Pay To The Order Of: _____ $ [   ]

_____ Dollars

America United Bank

memo: _____   Signature: _____

I: 575864996■:   II■ 758969981I   0873

Date
October 16, 2018

Company
Ace Tennis Club

Amount
$30.50

Memo
November
Tennis

YMBA Student
4 Success Blvd.
Beautiful, State 98765 USA
info@ymbagroup.com

58-6499/5758   874

Date _____

Pay To The Order Of: _____ $ [   ]

_____ Dollars

America United Bank

memo: _____   Signature: _____

I: 575864996■:   II■ 758969981I   0874

Date
October 21, 2018

Company
TSHS Book Store

Amount
$25.82

Memo
History Books

YMBA Student
4 Success Blvd.
Beautiful, State 98765 USA
info@ymbagroup.com

58-6499/5758   875

Date _____

Pay To The Order Of: _____ $ [   ]

_____ Dollars

America United Bank

memo: _____   Signature: _____

I: 575864996■:   II■ 758969981I   0875

APPLY

Record The Payment

After a check is written the details must be written so the check writer can keep track of the balance that remains in the bank account. A check writer can choose between a paper check register to record payments (shown below), or a computer software program. Let us look at the check register below. The checks you wrote on the prior page are shown in the register below. Notice the check number, the date the check was written, who you gave the check to, and the amount paid are recorded. The **last column** is called a running balance. **The running balance is the amount of money in the account after each check is deducted or when a deposit is made to the account**

Why is the running balance important?

Consider this scenario: A check was written on October 7 to Clong Electric for $64.31. Clong Electric may not deposit the check for a week or longer. The writer of a check has to consider the money as spent so checks are not written at a later time for an account that is unable to pay the funds. The person or company the check was written to will deposit the check into their own bank account. The funds transfer will be arranged between the banks. If the funds are not available in the check writers account at the bank will notify the holder of the check that the payment could not be honored (paid). The check

will be an NSF check (non-sufficient funds). There is not enough money in the account to pay the check. When a check is not paid due to a lack of funds a fee is most likely charged to the check writer by their bank.

Number	Date	Transaction	Withdrawal		√	Deposit		$ 284.00	
873	10/7	Clong Electric September/2014	64	31				219	69
874	10/16	Ace Soccer November/2014	30	50				189	19
--	10/20	Babysitting on October 19, 2014				22	00	211	19
875	10/21	TSHS Book Store	25	82				185	37
	10/24								
	10/25					25	00		
--	10/31								
877	11/7	Dentist Dr. Gold	39	00				122	37
878	11/12	SatTV	30	00				92	37
--	11/21	Babysitting on Nov. 21, 2014				40	00	132	37

Enter the items below in the check register.

Check Number 876 is written to Dr. Smart for $50.00 on 10/24.

On 10/25 a check is received for $25.00 from your grandmother.

On 10/31 the bank issues $1 for interest on the account.

APPLY

18

The Drawing Board

Complete the checks using the information next to the first two stars below. Next, enter the details for all three stars below into the page 18 check register. Last, return to this page to answer question 3.

1.

YMBA Student
4 Success Blvd.
Beautiful, State 98765 USA
ymbagroup@outlook.com

58-6499/5758   877

Date _____

Pay To The Order Of: _____ $ [   ]

_____ Dollars

America United Bank

memo: _____ Signature: _____

I: 575864996■:   II■ 7589699811   0877

2.

YMBA Student
4 Success Blvd.
Beautiful, State 98765 USA
ymbagroup@outlook.com

58-6499/5758   878

Date _____

Pay To The Order Of: _____ $ [   ]

_____ Dollars

America United Bank

memo: _____ Signature: _____

I: 575864996■:   II■ 7589699811   0878

💡 You attend the dentist, Dr. Gold, and pay with a check the full amount due of $39.00 on November 7, 2018.

💡 Your cable television bill to SatTV arrives and you owe $30. You write and mail the check on November 12, 2018.

💡 You babysit on November 21, 2018 and deposit the amount of $40.

3. What is the new balance in your register?    $ [_____]

THINK

Money On The Move

A customer may choose to pay for a good or service using a check. A check is a written promise from the bank of the person who wrote the check to the person they give the check to that there is money in the account to make the payment. The banking customer will only write a check when there is enough money in their bank account to pay the amount of the check. This will allow the bank to honor (pay) the check when it is deposited for payment. For this reason, it is vital to keep an accurate record of your bank balance.

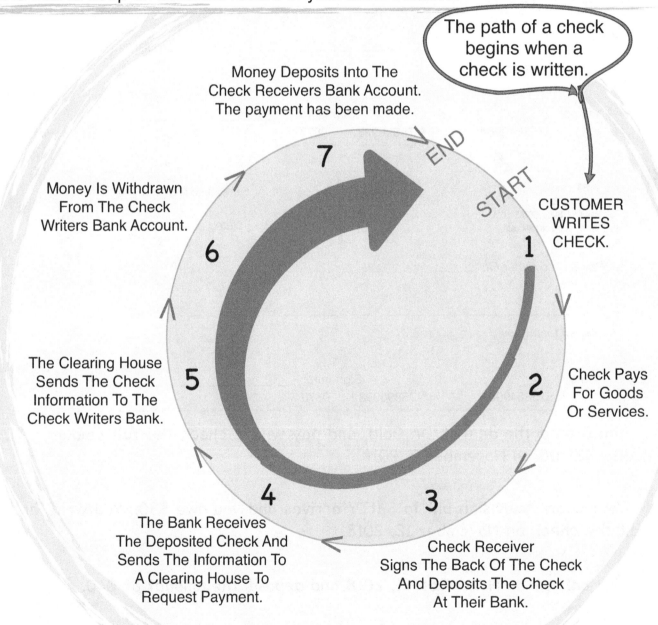

The path of a check begins when a check is written.

Money Deposits Into The Check Receivers Bank Account. The payment has been made.

7

START

END

Money Is Withdrawn From The Check Writers Bank Account.

6

CUSTOMER WRITES CHECK.

1

Check Pays For Goods Or Services.

2

The Clearing House Sends The Check Information To The Check Writers Bank.

5

4

3

The Bank Receives The Deposited Check And Sends The Information To A Clearing House To Request Payment.

Check Receiver Signs The Back Of The Check And Deposits The Check At Their Bank.

www.YMBAgroup.com

The Drawing Board

Number the items below in the correct order to show the path of a check.

Dear Bank Customer,

Regrettably, it appears that a check you recently wrote was for an amount greater than the amount in your bank account. As a result, the check number 816 for $425.00 was not paid.

The bank has charged your bank checking account $25 for the bounced check due to having insufficient funds to pay the check.

The amount of $25 was deducted from your account this morning. Be sure to note the $25 deduction in your check register.

Sincerely,

Mr. Brown Pants
Your Bank Manager

☐ Money Deposits Into The Check Receivers Bank Account. Payment has been made.

☐ Check Writers Bank Withdraws Money From The Check Writers Bank Account

☐ Check Receivers Bank Sends Check Information To A Clearing House

☐ CUSTOMER WRITES CHECK

☐ The Clearing House Sends The Check Information To The Check Writers Bank

☐ Check Receiver Signs The Check Back To Endorse The Check And Deposits Check At A Bank

☐ Check Pays For Goods Or Services

STRATEGIZE

www.YMBAgroup.com

Types Of Payment

A common business goal is to make a profit. A profit is when a company has money after all the expenses that are due have been paid. A business will seek to sell products and services to customers to help make a profit. The sale of products helps a company hire more employees, invest in new research, improve their operations and more. To help increase their sales a company makes it as simple as possible for a customer to complete a purchase by offering different payment options. As you read the chart below consider which payment option would be most commonly selected by the customer for which type of purchase.

Method of Payment	Benefit	Risk
Trade	Get something you want in trade for something you don't need.	May be difficult to return due to a problem.
Cash	You own the item 100% at the time of purchase. No interest charged.	If misplaced and lost not possible to recover.
ATM Card	No need to carry large amounts of cash and risk it being lost.	Easy to overspend if not carefully tracking spending.
Electronic Payment	A solution for paying larger dollar amounts.	If sending funds by wire there may be extra costs.
Check	Creates a clear paper history of who you paid, how much and when. Will also show where the check was deposited.	Once paid may be difficult to return or receive an amount paid back to your account.
Credit Card	Easy to shop on the internet. Can dispute a charge and a credit card company can help determine if the charge is accurate.	Internet fees will need to be paid back, in addition to the charged amount.
Unsecured Loan (family)	Flexible terms that work for you. No check of your credit report.	Possible cause of family disagreements.
Secured Loan (bank)	Cash you need without any involvement in your relationships with family and friends.	Little to no flexibility in repayment terms.

The Drawing Board

Consider the following purchase scenarios. In the space provided indicate the most likely type of payment. Choose payment types from the toolbox below.

TOOLBOX

Trade	ATM Card	Check	Unsecured Loan (family)
Cash	Electronic Payment	Credit Card	Secured Loan (bank)

1. You visit the dentist and pay an $85 invoice. _____

2. You are going out with friends later and would like to have $20 cash from your bank account. _____

3. You are planning on going to college and need to pay for the first semester of classes. _____

4. After school you stop for a slice of pizza. _____

5. You finished book seven in a series. Your friend has not read book seven, but just finished book 5. _____

6. Your favorite video game just broke. You would like a new one, but have to wait eight weeks to have enough allowance money to afford a new game. _____

7. You are on the internet at an online store and found a wonderful birthday gift for your mother. _____

8. Your family just bought a new house. _____

EXPLORE

www.YMBAgroup.com

Reasons To Save Your Money

Buy A Home	**Purchase A Car**
Pay For College	**Go On A Vacation** **Plan For Retirement**

A bank wants people to be their customer and open savings accounts at their location. To encourage people to save money at a bank a customer receives an offer of interest (money). How does a bank benefit when people deposit money in the bank?
A bank uses the money deposited by some customers to be able to loan money to other customers. A bank will collect interest when a loan is given to customers.

Consider this example:

A bank welcomes a new savings account customer.

The customer makes an $8,000 deposit to open the account.

The money in the account will earn an annual interest rate of 2%.

The 2% interest rate per year is the banks return to the customer.

The same day the bank approves a different customer for an $8,000 car loan.

The bank will charge a 5% interest rate per year to the car loan customer.

The bank will earn a profit equal to 3% per year on the $8,000 car loan.

A Simple Car Loan Scenario.

(1) What is 5% of $8,000?

Step 1: Convert 5% to a decimal. Remove the percent sign and move left two spaces, add a decimal. 5% = .05

Step 2: Multiply $8,000 x .05 = $400

Step 3: The bank will earn $400 in interest a year on the car loan.

Did you know when an interest rate is per year it is called an Annual Interest Rate.

The Drawing Board

Interest is the added money to your deposit or investment. The cash in an account is called principal. Interest is generally added monthly, quarterly or annually and added to the principal. Compute the amount of interest earned on the investments below.

Principal x Interest Rate x Time = Interest Earned In That Time

8,000 x .02 x 1 year = $160

Pump Up Interest

1. A savings account has a $500 balance for one year with an interest rate of 2%. How much interest will be added to the account by the bank?

   $500 x .02 x 1 year = $ _____

2. A checking account has a $2,000 balance for two years with an interest rate of 1%. How much interest will be added to the account by the bank? $ _____

3. A college savings account has a $4,000 balance for one year with an interest rate of 3%. How much interest will be added to the account by the bank? $ _____

4. In a second savings account you have an $800 balance that earns 3% interest for three years. How much interest will be added to the account by the bank? $ _____

5. How much interest did you earn in total on all investments?

   $ _____

APPLY

www.YMBAgroup.com

Structure Of A Company

Your friend Buddy is thinking of starting a business.

There are different ways a company can be organized.

Buddy asks you to go together to visit the accountant to consider the options.

The accountant explains that there are four general options to form a company. (1) Sole Proprietorship - this has one owner and a generally simple business plan. (2) Partnership - two or more owners and a business plan with agreements between the owners in a written format. (3) Limited Liability Company (known as an LLC) - owners of an LLC are known as members and have some benefits of a corporation. (4) A Corporation - owners are known as shareholders. The shareholders are not personally sued; the corporation is sued. The corporation pays corporate taxes.

A Corporation name usually MUST End With One Of The Following Words
- Co.
- Company
- Inc.
- Incorporated
- Corp.
- Corporation

What is it to be INCORPORATED? A corporation in the USA is registered with a state as a business. The corporation has shareholders, not owners. Each shareholder owns shares (a part) of the company. An incorporated business is also referred to as a corporation.

A SUBSIDIARY is a separately incorporated company that is owned by another incorporated company.

A DIVISION is part of an incorporated company.

HOSTILE TAKEOVER of a company - happens when a group of people convince stock owners of a company to vote for new company executives (leaders). By doing this the company is managed and run by different people, often with a different set of ideas for how the business should be managed. The current leaders of the company generally do not know when this is about to happen and is considered a hostile takeover.

A company **BUY OUT** happens when one company purchases enough stock in another company to have the majority of votes. As a result, the company that owns the stock majority can win any vote or election. In this way, the company that owns the majority of stock will win all voted upon decisions in a company.

Listed below are two different company organizational charts. The first company, Razzle Dazzle Toy Company has three divisions. The second company, Sun 2 Sea 2 Snow Travel Inc. has three subsidiaries. Be creative! List three possible ideas for division names in the Razzle Dazzle Toy Company and three ideas that could be subsidiary names for the Sun 2 Sea 2 Snow Travel company.

Division Organizational Chart

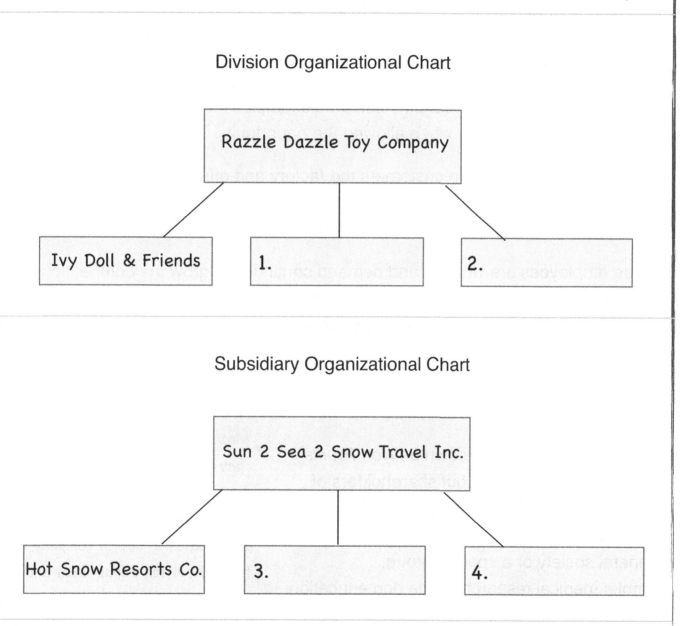

Razzle Dazzle Toy Company

Ivy Doll & Friends

1.

2.

Subsidiary Organizational Chart

Sun 2 Sea 2 Snow Travel Inc.

Hot Snow Resorts Co.

3.

4.

A MERGER is when two businesses come together.
An ACQUISITION is when one company buys another business and keeps only some parts of the purchased company.

CREATE

Laissez-Faire

An idea discussed by author Adam Smith in the 1700s was known as laissez-faire, pronounced (lay-zay-fair). The concept of laissez-faire is that a marketplace should allow a business to operate with only a small amount of decision making being made by the government.

During the early 1800s in England, and the late 1800's in the United States, there was a limited number of business decisions being made by the government on behalf of the business owner. Business owners had a lot of freedom to try new ideas. The marketplace during each of these periods had extensive growth and innovation.

These growth times for the economy serve as examples that a business owner will see ways to grow their company when allowed the opportunity.

When a business gains more customers the factory and office production will increase to meet the production demand for the product. This causes an increase in employment so the company will have enough products to satisfy the demand.

As more employees are working and demand continues to grow the competition between brands increases. Competition motivates a business to innovate. New inventions are often developed in competitive markets.

This style of market management has a high amount of freedom. A laissez-faire market has a limited amount of rules and reporting requested of the owners and employees.

Not-For-Profit - are also known as *Non-Profits*. An incorporated business, but shareholders of this business type do not receive dividends. The non-profit goal is to function for the benefit of general society or a specific group. Example: medical research, guide dog education.

Most non-profit businesses do not pay certain taxes to the federal or state governments. To qualify for this benefit a non-profit needs to be approved as a "501-C" company by the federal tax department known as the Internal Revenue Service. (IRS)

For-Profit - The opposite of a not for profit is called a for-profit company. The goal of a for-profit business is to make money so they can have money to invest in the business, grow the company, and expand products. The majority of for-profit businesses are motivated by wanting to expand a good or service to have a growing company.

Solve the word search using the words in the toolbox below.

TOOLBOX

market	laissez	freedom	jobs	taxes	production
economy	faire	innovate	profit	company	demand

```
n  x  t  a  x  e  s  z  e  f
t  o  v  e  e  k  e  p  t  r
i  f  i  x  k  s  o  k  a  e
f  j  a  t  s  r  c  l  v  e
o  t  o  i  c  m  a  j  o  d
r  i  a  b  r  u  t  m  n  o
p  l  y  k  s  e  d  o  n  m
e  c  o  n  o  m  y  o  i  i
i  y  n  a  p  m  o  c  r  x
d  e  m  a  n  d  b  y  o  p
```

Solve the cryptogram below.

The letters Y M B A and F U N have already been solved.

A	B	C	D	E	F	G	H	I	J	K	L	M	N	O	P	Q	R	S	T	U	V	W	X	Y	Z
19	20				24							25	4						11	20				8	

$$\frac{}{17}\ \frac{}{1}\ \frac{M}{25}\ \frac{}{14}\ \frac{}{21}\ \frac{}{18}\ \frac{I}{2}\ \frac{}{18}\ \frac{I}{2}\ \frac{}{1}\ \frac{N}{4}$$

$$\frac{M}{25}\ \frac{}{1}\ \frac{}{18}\ \frac{}{2}\ \frac{}{23}\ \frac{A}{19}\ \frac{}{18}\ \frac{}{21}\ \frac{}{10}$$

$$\frac{A}{19}\ \frac{B}{20}\ \frac{U}{11}\ \frac{}{10}\ \frac{}{2}\ \frac{N}{}\ \frac{}{21}\ \frac{}{10}\ \frac{}{10}$$

$$\frac{}{18}\ \frac{}{1}\ \frac{N}{2}\ \frac{}{4}\ \frac{}{4}\ \frac{}{1}\ \frac{V}{20}\ \frac{}{19}\ \frac{}{18}\ \frac{}{21}$$

STRATEGIZE

Rules In The Marketplace

There are many different market styles for buying and selling. A factor that has a large influence on how buyers and sellers come together in the marketplace involves the amount of involvement between the government and the business owners. The level of government involvement in business decisions can range from very low (capitalism) to very high (communism). Generally less government involvement results in a greater number of inventions and buyer choices.

Capitalism - A capitalist marketplace has most businesses owned by people rather than the government. The owners of a company make most of the decisions about how the business will operate. How much the owner and the employees get paid is often based on the sales profit from the company products. The success of this marketplace is based on the idea people want to work to be successful and have pride in a good day's work. A business in this marketplace has a high risk of failing, but if successful, a high investment return.

Socialism - A socialist marketplace operates under a high level of government monitoring and decision making on behalf of the business owners. This marketplace will try to give all members goods and services to meet their needs. Businesses in this marketplace achieve a common equal level of success and have a little chance for personal success beyond the community average. Most decisions are government made. Low risk, little personal succes

Communism - This style of market management has a high amount of data reporting and restriction with a low level of freedom. One specific business will not thrive in this market system. Communism market systems focus on all members of the market being equal and in doing so reduces the individual motivations to learn, succeed, and innovate. Very few inventions, discoveries or theories evolve from members of a communist market system.

The Drawing Board

Marketplace Fun

Laissez-Faire   Socialism   For-Profit Company

Communism   Capitalism   Non-Profit Company

Imagine you were just brushing your teeth and ran out of toothpaste. **Circle one** of the words in the toolbox to describe the marketplace where you shop. Next, **create a comic strip** to share a creative, funny story about the trip from your home to the store to purchase a new tube of toothpaste. Be sure to **include details** about your marketplace as you describe your trip to the store.

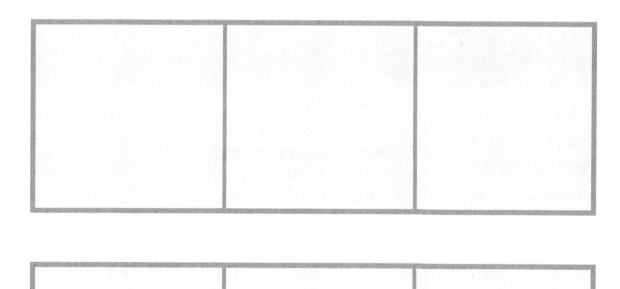

CREATE

Corporate Stock

There are different ways to organize and set up a company. One of these ways is to register as a corporation. A corporation is the only type of business that may offer shares of stock for sale. The shares of stock are made available to purchase on a stock market to investors.

When an investor chooses to buy **stock** in a company their purchase adds money to the funds available for corporate spending. There is no guarantee a stock purchase will be paid back to the investor. Since the stock purchase amount is not required to be paid back to the investor the money becomes part of the **EQUITY** of a company. An investor who purchases stock may receive a dividend payment. The amount of a dividend, if paid, will vary since payments to investors are based on company profits.

The opposite of investing in the company equity happens when an investor purchases a bond. A **bond** provides money to the company, but it must be paid back to the investor. Since the bond needs to be paid back by the company the expense is added to the **DEBT** of a corporation. Debt is the bills a corporation needs to pay. Investors choose bonds as a low-risk investment since the corporation has to pay back the bond owner.

> Stock purchases are EQUITY in a corporation, no requirement to be paid back.
> A bond needs to be paid back by the company, so it is part of the DEBT of a corporation

"No Par Value" means the price of one share of stock is determined by the amount investors are willing to pay for a share of the stock. The more investors want to purchase, the more demand it creates. More demand will make the stock price increase. If there is less demand, the stock price will decrease.

"Par Value" is also known as "Face Value" and is the stock price that the company chose is printed on the front of the stock certificate.

Market Leader
Blue chip stocks are often a market leader business with a high percentage of shoppers in the industry buying their products.

Voting Rights
Common stock owners are usually able to vote in company elections for the Board of Directors and other topics. The number of votes a shareholder has is equal to the number of shares they own.
If a shareholder can not be at the voting location they may choose to **Vote By Proxy** and allow someone to vote on their behalf.

Blue-Chip Stocks
Corporate stocks may be classified as a blue chip stock when they are considered less risky. A company is considered less risky when they have been in business for many years with a history of consistent results. A blue-chip company will also approve to pay dividends to shareholders on a regular schedule.

Majority Shareholder
When one shareholder owns 51% or more of the stock in a company.

The Drawing Board

An incorporated company will likely have a Board of Directors. Imagine the Board of Directors for each of your stock investments voted to approve the payment of common stock dividends. The questions below show the total dollar amount to be shared among the common stock shareholders as a dividend. First, calculate the dividend to be paid per share by using division. Next, compute your total dividend amount by multiplying the dividend by your number of shares.

1. P2A Games Incorporated approved a total dividend payout of $21,000. The company has a total of 14,000 shares outstanding.

   $21,000 divided by 14,000 = $1.50

   Dividend Per Share: $ _____$1.50_____

   Total Dividends Paid To Me: $ _$1.50 x 1000 = $1,500_

Your Common Stock Portfolio	
Company	Shares You Own
P2A Games Incorporated	1000 Shares
Sloppy Shirt Company	20 Shares
Health Ye, Health Ye Cereal Co.	100 Shares
Red, White and Glue Corp.	400 Shares
New Snow Each Week Resorts Inc.	50 Shares

2. Sloppy Shirt Company approved a total dividend payout of $12,600. The company has a total of 3,000 shares outstanding.

   Dividend Per Share: $ _____   Total Dividends Paid To Me: $ _____

3. Health Ye, Health Ye Cereal Co. approved a total dividend payout of $30,000. The company has a total of 15,000 shares outstanding.

   Dividend Per Share: $ _____   Total Dividends Paid To Me: $ _____

4. Red, white and Glue Corp. approved a total dividend payout of $16,400. The company has a total of 8,000 shares outstanding.

   Dividend Per Share: $ _____   Total Dividends Paid To Me: $ _____

5. New Snow Each Week Resorts Inc. approved a total dividend payout of $5,250. The company has a total of 3000 shares outstanding.

Dividend Per Share: $ _____   Total Dividends Paid To Me: $ _____

EXPLORE

The Stock Exchange

A stock exchange is a place where investors may purchase shares in a company. There are many stock exchanges located around the world in locations including London, England; Tokyo, Japan; Toronto, Canada; Shanghai, China and Zurich, Switzerland. The oldest, and perhaps best known, is the New York Stock Exchange (abbreviated NYSE) and located in New York City, New York.

Each stock type has benefits. An investor may select either common stock or preferred stock. The stock type an investor chooses will depend on their investment style and strategy, as well as their long-term and short-term goals.

Common Stock gives the owner who purchased the stock the right to vote on some company topics. The common stockholder will receive dividends (money) only when the company performs well enough to have a profit that the company decides to distribute as dividends to investors. Common stockholders receive their dividends after preferred stock holders receive their dividends.

Preferred Stockholders do not participate with a vote in elections and company decisions. A preferred stockholder does get paid a dividend before the common stockholders. Also, if a company declares itself bankrupt, the preferred stockholders will be paid before the common stockholders receive payments.

Earnings Per Share (EPS) = The dividend paid per share of common stock. When a corporation has money available after all bills and expenses are paid the company is said to have made a profit. From the profit the company will pay preferred stock holders a dividend. A corporation may vote to save the money or the corporation may decide to use a portion of their profit to pay common stock holders a dividend.

When To Buy Stock? When To Sell Stock?

Have you ever heard the expression, "Buy low, sell high" regarding shares of stock? Buy low refers to purchasing a stock when the stock price is low. Sell high refers to selling the stock when the price is high. For example, if a stock is bought at $23 a share then sold at $43 a share, the buyer would receive $20 more than paid per share. If the buyer had ten shares of stock they just made $200! ($20 x 10 shares)

Complete the worksheet below with a friend. First, ask your friend to select a word for each blank that is in the category shown below the blank. After all blanks have an answer read the page aloud to your friend.

_____ Incorporated has just completed its red herring to tell
          Noun

_____ about the stock the company is going to offer for sale.
  Type of animal, plural

_____ your phone alerts you a call is coming in on your phone.
   Funny sound

Your best friend, _____ , invited you to meet at the
                        Friends name

_____ to read the stock details in the red herring together.
     Place

When you arrive you are _____ to see the local _____
                              Emotion   Verb ending in -ing

group _____ on their _____ . Your friend
        Verb ending in -ing   Body part, plural

arrives and you call out your best friend secret code sound "_____"
                                                                  Funny sound

to get their attention.

As you are both sitting on a _____ reading the red herring
                                Thing to sit on

many exciting details of future company plans are revealed. For example,

the company will release _____ _____
                              Number   Small, tiny object, plural

down a steep hill for a contest. The winner will need to successfully

_____ over at least _____ of the objects. The
  Verb, singular   Number

contest will repeat until there is a winner.

You and your best friend agree to invest in the stock and say

good-bye with your secret _____ handshake.
                              Animal

A red herring gives details about a new company stock.

CREATE

Bull Market - A market is a "bull market" when the average price of a stock on the stock market has an increasing price. When the average of stock prices increase it is considered a growing economy and a growing market.

Bear Market - A market is a "bear market" when the stocks that are traded on the stock market have an average decreasing price. The decreasing price is considered a reduction in the number of investors seeking to buy stocks and bonds.

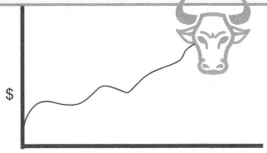

$

$

Hint: Imagine a bull pulling a rope up a hill. The rope shows the stock prices getting higher.

Hint: Imagine a bear lying down on the ground for the winter to hibernate. Lying down on the ground shows the stock prices going lower.

Red Herring - When a corporation decides it will be traded on a stock exchange an information book called a red herring is created for potential investors. The red herring will give potential investors information about the company stock. The name red herring is because the front cover of the book is often printed in red ink.

Neigh! Neigh!

Stag - A term used to refer to an investor who buys a company IPO as soon as it is available. The investor plans to sell it soon, in the short term, for a profit. A stag investment is when a stock is sold for a profit shortly after it is bought.

Quack! Quack!

IPO
Initial Public Offer
The first time a company offers stock for sale.

Lame Duck - In finance the term "lame duck" refers to a person or business that is not able to pay the bills. In politics the term refers to a person at the end of their elected office term after the person who will take over has already been elected.

www.YMBAgroup.com

The Drawing Board

Stocks overall move up or move down in the stock market.
In a bull market average stock prices are going up.
In a bear market average stock prices are going down.

Examine the average stock prices shown below for June, July, August and September.
Circle **bull** or **bear** if the stock prices trending are part of a bull, or a bear, market.

	Jun	Jul	Aug	Sep	Circle One	
. Stock Price History:	$18.14	$18.60	$19.10	$19.50	Bull	Bear
. Stock Price History:	$59.00	$63.20	$65.00	$68.12	Bull	Bear
. Stock Price History:	$17.43	$16.90	$14.10	$12.80	Bull	Bear
. Stock Price History:	$117.40	$111.46	$104.71	$99.25	Bull	Bear
. Stock Price History:	$19.00	$22.60	$28.30	$29.40	Bull	Bear
. Stock Price History:	$15.00	$13.50	$13.40	$11.80	Bull	Bear
. Stock Price History:	$11.90	$11.10	$10.60	$10.00	Bull	Bear

INVESTIGATE

www.YMBAgroup.com

Savings Bonds

An investment available from a company or government is called a bond.
A bond has a very low risk to the investor, so the interest rates paid are small.
The value of the bond available for investors varies, known as par value.
The bond will offer additional money to the person who owns the bond.
The bond will also pay back the original investment cost to buy the bond.
The bond will be paid back at a future date, known as the date of maturity.
The amount to be paid in the future is known as the par value.
The extra money to be paid to the bond owner is known as interest.
The date in the future the bond will be paid back is known as the maturity date.

> A bond is purchased from a company or government by an investor.
> The bond has a par value to be paid, plus interest, on the bond maturity date.

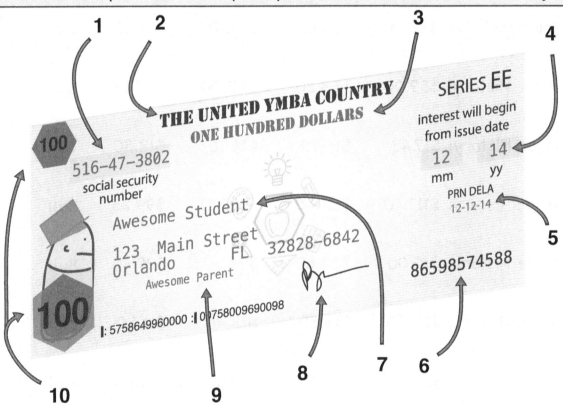

1. Social Security Number of the person who will own the savings bond.

2. The company or government that issued the savings bond and will be paying interest to the owner.

3. The value of the savings bond spelled out in words.

4. The month and year when the savings bond interest earnings begin.

5. The date the savings bond was printed.

6. The bond serial number. This number is unique to each savings bond.

7. The name and street address of the owner of the savings bond.

8. The signature or name of a company representative that issued the bond.

9. If the savings bond owner is under 18 years old a parent or guardian will be listed here.

10. The maturity value of the savings bond.

The Drawing Board

Imagine it is your birthday. As a gift you just received a savings bond. Enter a number from the list at the bottom of the page into the square box to explain and identify the parts of the savings bond.

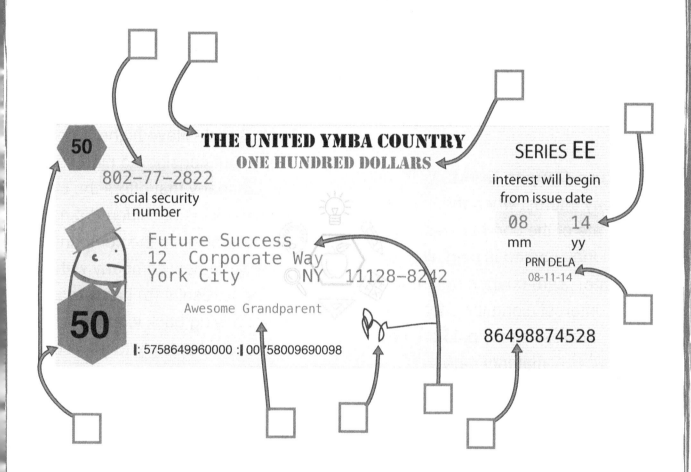

1. The maturity value of the savings bond.

2. The signature or name of a company representative that issued the bond.

3. The government that issued the savings bond and will be paying interest to the owner.

4. Social Security Number of person who will own the savings bond.

5. Since the savings bond owner is under 18 years old a parent or guardian.

6. The name and street address of the owner of the savings bond.

7. The date the savings bond was printed.

8. The value of the savings bond spelt out in words.

9. The month and year when the savings bond interest earnings begin.

10. The bond serial number. This number is unique to each savings bond.

APPLY

Bond Types

There are many different types of bonds. Bonds offer investors various combinations of interest earned and payment terms. A bond is considered less risky than buying corporate stock or investing in a mutual fund since a bond investment is considered very likely to be paid back to the investor (buyer).

An additional benefit of a bond is that if a company declares bankruptcy bondholders are the first of the investors that are owed money to be paid. After the bondholders are paid the next group to be paid are preferred stockholders. The common stockholders are then paid the amounts they are owed if the corporation has any more money.

Zero-Coupon Bond - Will only pay interest when the maturity rate of the bond arrives. The money earned is paid all at one time. Zero-coupon means zero interest along the way, and interest is only paid on the maturity date.

Junk Bond - Have higher interest rates but considered high risk. The company that offers the bond to investors is considered a risky investment since the company is either (a) a new company with no business results (b) has a record of not paying back loans or (c) is considered unlikely to succeed.

DIFFERENT TYPES OF BONDS

Floating Rate Bond - Some bonds do not have a set interest rate when they are purchased. The company offering the bond will let the buyer know that the interest rate will vary. An interest rate that varies means that each month the bond will return a different percent of the money invested.

Asset-Backed Bond - The company offering the bond tells the buyer that if for some reason they do not have the cash to pay when the term is up that they will sell a specific asset. The money from the sale of the asset will be then be used to pay the bond.

Imagine each savings bond had a family of its own. Using the bond types shown in the toolbox below match the family vacation details that would best describe the family of that type of savings bond.

1. My family - When my family and I go on vacation we like to try a different adventure each day. We let our friends and family know that we have no plans from one time to the next. That each day will be something new. They just never know what pictures we will share next! If my family and I were a savings bond we would be a _____ bond.

2. My family - When my family and I go on vacation we stay very active. We like to skydive over mountains, rollerblade with one skate and pet exotic animals that have massive teeth. We are new to traveling, but we enjoy driving without a map and just following to road. Sometimes we find the hotel without a map or directions. (A few nights we ended up camping rather than staying at a hotel). If my family and I were a savings bond we would be a _____ bond.

3. My family - When my family and I go on vacation we enjoy taking a few years to plan the trip. We do not travel while we wait for the vacation to arrive. But, we have fun talking about the trip and making plans for when the trip date arrives. If my family and I were a savings bond we would be a _____ bond.

4. My family - When my family and I go on vacation we make a deal that if we each do not have a fantastic vacation that we will plan a new vacation when we get back home. The backup vacation plan helps each of us have a bit less worry about each detail of the vacation. If one vacation is not an awesome adventure, then we always have a back up plan! If my family and I were a savings bond we would be a _____ bond.

BOND TYPES   TOOLBOX

Zero-Coupon Bond	Floating Rate Bond
Junk Bond	Asset-Backed Bond

EXPLORE

A mutual fund is a group of stocks and bonds placed together into one investment account to help an investor diversify to reduce risk. When mutual funds are grouped together the fund is named to give investors an idea of the risk strategy. Examples are, *Florida Low-Risk Mutual Fund* or the *Texas Growth Fund.*

Benefit #1

A mutual fund helps an investor easily choose a combination of stocks and bonds to meet their individual goal and investment risk style. The person or company offering the mutual fund investment researched and evaluated the corporations that are part of the fund. As a result of being researched by a professional, an investor can save the time of having to research each stock or bond on their own. Mutual funds are classified as high risk, high to medium risk, medium risk, medium to low risk, or low ri

Benefit #2

A mutual fund helps an investor achieve a diversified strategy. Diversified refers to the investments in a mutual fund being placed in different types of investments. If one stock in the mutual fund does not return a profit to the investor, perhaps the other investments in the fund will have a profit to balance out the overall results.

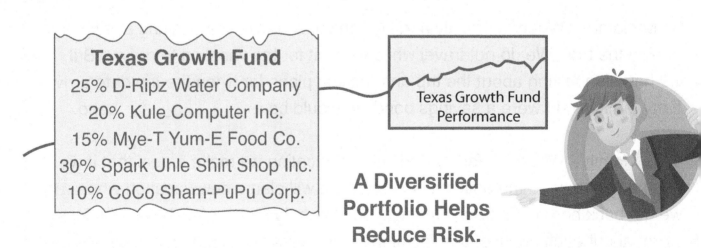

Texas Growth Fund
25% D-Ripz Water Company
20% Kule Computer Inc.
15% Mye-T Yum-E Food Co.
30% Spark Uhle Shirt Shop Inc.
10% CoCo Sham-PuPu Corp.

Texas Growth Fund Performance

A Diversified Portfolio Helps Reduce Risk.

Diversification happens when an investor chooses a variety of different stocks or bonds to purchase. The goal of diversification is to balance out a sudden decrease ir the value of one investment. For example, consider a mutual fund that has stocks fro the industries of utilities, real estate, new technology and medicine. If the stock for the new technology company decreases from $23.50 a share to $14.80 a share the value of that investment will decrease. However, the value of the overall investment can stay the same, or even increase, depending on the results of the other investmen

Would you select an aggressive strategy with high-risk investments?
Do you prefer a conservative investment strategy with a low-risk of loss?
Perhaps you prefer a combination of high-risk and low-risk investments?

As you read each item below circle yes, no, or maybe, to indicate which you would choose. "Yes" if you would make the same decision, "Maybe" if you would consider making the decision, and "No" if you would not make the decision.

1. I would invest in a mutual fund that has a high risk of not being profitable, but if profitable would double my investment.   No   Maybe   Yes

2. I would purchase stock in a new company.   No   Maybe   Yes

3. I would loan money without having a written agreement signed by the person receiving the money.   No   Maybe   Yes

4. I would purchase 100 shares of stock in a company at a price of $11.85 a share that I did not research.   No   Maybe   Yes

5. I would open a savings account at a new bank in town.   No   Maybe   Yes

6. I would buy a car on the internet without having time to see or inspect the car before paying.   No   Maybe   Yes

7. I would pay $5 to play a bingo game with a $1,000 prize.   No   Maybe   Yes

8. I would mail a credit card payment three days before the date the payment is due to be received by the company.   No   Maybe   Yes

Low Risk = 8 – 14 points
Medium Risk = 15 – 19 points
High Risk = 20 – 24 points

What is your investment style?

For each "Yes" add 3 points.
For each "Maybe" add 2 points.
For each "No" add 1 point.

INVESTIGATE

Invest In Your Future

Would you like to have $10,000 in 12 years? Sure, right? Did you know that investing $60 a month (that is just $2 a day) into a savings account that earns 2% interest a month will give you $10,000 in savings in 12 years?

There are many different ways to invest money. Popular savings options include a savings account, a 529 college savings account, and a 401k retirement account.

529 College Savings Account

A 529 account will save college funds on behalf of another person, or someone may save for their future college expenses. The amount earned in a 529 are taxed differently and often have tax benefits. The 529 accounts, like most investment accounts, have simplified the process of making scheduled automatic deposits into the account. Consistent investing of any amount is the key to accumulating (building up) a balance in any account.

401k Retirement Investment Account

A 401k investment account is one way a person may save money for their retirement. The investment is taken from their work earnings regularly. Since the amounts are invested in the 401k come directly out of their paycheck the amount they invest does not get taxed. When funds are withdrawn (taken out) of the account by the person who invested the money during their retirement taxes would likely not apply.

Did you know? A popular benefit offered by a business to the employees is a match to the employee deposit into their 401k account?

$ = $

For example, if an employee deposits $20 a week to the 401k account their employer will also deposit $20. This will result in $40 a week added to the employee 401k account.

Do you think the *529 account* or the *401k account* has a better set of benefits? Why?

THINK

www.YMBAgroup.com

Compute the balance for the following investment descriptions:

1. Clara receives an account statement in the mail. The statement shows the total amount she deposited as $2,640. It also shows the interest earned is 5%. What is the total balance of her 529 college savings account?

$2,640 x .05 = $132

Amount Deposited: $2,640.
Interest Earned: + $132.
The total account balance is $2,772.

2. Ella has been investing all her childcare money in a 529 college savings account. She has a total balance of $850 with 4% interest earned on the $850. What is total balance of her 529 college savings account?

3. Cody has a 401k retirement account at his job. He has been investing $100 a month into his account. His employer has a 100% match to the employee contributions. After one year what is the total balance deposited into his account?

4. Ken has been adding $40 a month to the 529 college savings account of his brother Sven for the past six months. Sven receives his investment statement and notices the $500 he deposited, but also notices the balance shows an additional deposit. What is the total amount his account increased over the past six months?

5. Ruby has a 529 savings account with a balance of $6,000. She also has a 401k retirement account with a balance of $2,400. Both accounts are expected to earn 4% interest next year. If all goes as planned, what will be the balance in each account? What is the total balance of both accounts?

+ −
× ÷

COMPUTE

What Is Interest?

Interest is the money that is given in exchange for providing your funds to a bank, company, or government. When a customer makes a deposit, or invests money, the funds are then used by the company that received the funds to expand and grow. The bank, company or government will pay the investor a percent of the amount of money that was invested. Investors generally receive payments monthly, quarterly or yearly. The regular amounts paid on the investment are called earnings. Receiving (being given) earnings are an incentive for people to invest money.

Imagine you made a financial plan to invest $30 a month into your savings account that will earn 2% a year interest for ten years. Your account currently has $50 in the account. You would like to know how much interest will you earn after ten years? What will be the total amount in your account after ten years?

The formula to learn how much interest you will earn is:

Interest = Principal x Rate x Time

Step 1: Figure out how much money in total you will deposit into the account.
The deposit amount will be $30 a month for ten years. The total amount deposited is known as **PRINCIPAL**.   12 months in a year = 12 x 10 years = 120 month

Principal = $30 a month x 120 months = ⟨$3,600⟩ invested in 10 yea

Step 2: The interest the investment will earn is known as the **RATE**.

Rate = 2%   2% written as a decimal is (.0

Step 3: Since the investment *earns interest every year* identify how many years the money will be invested. The total length of time is called the **TIME** of investment.

Time = |10| yea

Interest = Principal x Rate x Time
Interest =   ⟨$3,600⟩ x(.02) x |10| years
Interest = $72   x 10 years
Interest = $720
Total Future Account Balance: $720 interest earned
                                + $3,600 invested
                                + $50 starting balance
                        ─────────────────────────
                        $4,370 account balance in 10 years

Great Job Saving!

Congratulations! You have become a wise investor and have been successful at saving some of your money. Find the solution to the three problems below. Add the three totals together to learn the total balance of your investments.

(see the example at the bottom of the prior page for a hint)

1. On January 1 of last year your savings account had a $200 balance. Your account earned 2% during the year. What is your savings account balance on December 31 of the same year?

2. On January 1 of last year you began a financial plan to invest $25 a month into your 529 college savings account. The account earned 5% interest for the year. What is your savings account balance on December 31 of the same year?

3. During the last year your family offered to pay you $2 a week for each week the chores were completed at the house. There are 52 weeks in a year. Two weeks you did not do chores. One week you were out of town so chores were not done during that week as well. You spent half of the chore money during the year. The other half you saved in a safe in your bedroom. What was the total amount of chore money you had as of December 31 last year?

4. How much do you have in total investments at the end of the year?

$ _____ + $ _____ + $ _____ = $ _____

The formula to know an amount of interest is:

Interest = Principal x Rate x Time

COMPUTE

What is a loan?

The person who borrows money is called the **borrower**.

The person who lends the money is called the **lender**.

The **borrower pays the lender** the amount they borrowed, **plus** an extra amount called **interest**.

Why would someone give their money as a loan?

When money is paid to someone with the expectation it will be paid back this is called a loan. When a friend or family member lends money it is often without interest. The incentive to loan the money is to offer assistance to a friend. When a bank or company lends money it is often with interest. The incentive to loan the money is that the bank or company believes they will get the money back, along with extra money, interest. The interest is the money the bank or company earned for giving the loan.

Why would someone agree to pay back an amount greater than they borrowed?

There are times when a purchase is made and a person does not have all the cash in their savings to pay for the item. Examples where a loan is useful may be to purchase a house or car and to enroll in college. Each of these require a large payment in advance so a buyer can borrow the money and pay the debt back over a period of time.

The time a borrower has to pay back borrowed funds is known as the term of the loan.

Lending Goals	Borrowing Goals
+ Positive customer feedback to help attract new customers.	+ Reliable payment terms.
+ To earn interest on the loan to help make a profit.	+ Accurate feedback and data shared on the credit report.
	+ Personal information not shared without permission.
+ To develop a reliable business reputation in the marketplace.	+ Money received when needed.

The Drawing Board

A service that a bank offers a customer is a money loan. When a customer decides to request a loan they will complete an application. The bank will review the application and examine the application details regarding the candidates work experience and credit report history. A final decision will be made as either "approved" or "denied". Approved indicates the person will receive the money from the bank. Denied indicates that the bank was not able to approve the loan and the customer will not receive the money.

For the scenarios below imagine you are the loan manager at Buck City Bank. Circle your loan decision next to each scenario as either approved or denied.

1. This credit report is better than __82__ % when compared to other credit reports.
   The length of employment has been __11__ years at the same job.
   The applicant will work __2__ days each month to earn the money to pay the loan.
   The applicant has used __10__ % of the credit limit available on their credit cards.

   APPROVED   **DENIED**

2. This credit report is better than __30__ % when compared to other credit reports.
   The length of employment has been __4__ years at the same job.
   The applicant will work __7__ days each month to earn the money to pay the loan.
   The applicant has used __75__ % of the credit limit available on their credit cards.

   APPROVED   **DENIED**

3. This credit report is better than __90__ % when compared to other credit reports.
   The length of employment has been __16__ years at the same job.
   The applicant will work __1__ day each month to earn the money to pay the loan.
   The applicant has used __12__ % of the credit limit available on their credit cards.

   APPROVED   **DENIED**

4. This credit report is better than __45__ % when compared to other credit reports.
   The length of employment has been __1__ year at the same job.
   The applicant will work __8__ days each month to earn the money to pay the loan.
   The applicant has used __80__ % of the credit limit available on their credit cards.

   APPROVED   **DENIED**

STRATEGIZE

The Invoice

An invoice shows the balance due to be paid by a customer. The invoice will also show the buyer the price of each item purchased and when the amount needs to be paid. The date the amount needs to be paid by is known as the due date. After the invoice is paid a customer receives a receipt to show payment was completed.

Tread and Family Auto Supplies, Incorporated

INVOICE NUMBER: 647

November 7, 2018

DUE DATE: DECEMBER 5, 2018

Quantity	Stock Number	Item Details	Technician Initials	Price Each
1	TIRE 64H	Standard road use	MBA	$79.99
1	ROAD SVC	Roadside tire change	MBA	$25.00

ROAD SIDE ASSISTANCE AVAILABLE
EVERY DAY ANY TIME
24/7
LOCATION
DALLAS, TX

Sub-Total	$104.99
State Sales Tax 7%	$7.35
Total	$112.34

Describe the event that caused the need for the customer to contact Tread and Family Auto Supplies according to the invoice above.

_____

_____

_____

_____

_____

INVESTIGAT

Basic math skills are needed in every business and even when making personal shopping or investment decisions. In the business world common questions include: What is the cost of purchasing these supplies? How should I price the product? How profitable is the company? Personal finance questions may include: How much interest does my savings account earn? How much interest am I paying on my car loan? How much should I save for college?

Consider numbers as having their own personal style. At times the data being studied may be a percentage, such as 75%. At other times the data may be a fraction, shown as $\frac{3}{4}$. A different piece of data may be .75, a decimal. Each of the three shown in this paragraph are equal to three-quarters of the whole.

FRACTION	PERCENT	DECIMAL
A corporation stock price has a value of $34\frac{3}{4}$.	The shipping box inventory has 50% remaining in stock.	The sales employees each worked 38.5 hours last week.

Fill in the blanks with equivalent fractions, decimals and percents.

	Fraction	Decimal	Percent
1.	$\frac{1}{2}$	☐	☐
2.	☐	.25	☐
3.	$\frac{4}{10}$	☐	☐
4.	☐	.8	75%

5. *Percent To Fraction:*

A Percent Is A Part Of 100.

$\frac{54}{100} = 54\%$ *Mean 54 Parts of the 100 Total Parts*

Decimal To Percent:

.25 = 2 5 = 25%

Move the decimal point two places right and add the "%" sgain for a percent.

Decimal To Fraction:

$.25 = \frac{25}{100}$

A decimal is part of a whole. Example: .99 + .01 = 1 whole = $\frac{100}{100}$

COMPUTE

www.YMBAgroup.com

The Cost of Credit Cards

A credit card is a responsibility. When you apply for a credit card you promise the company or bank that you will repay the amount you owe for your purchases. After completing an application for a credit card, you will be notified of the application decision. A decision is either approved or denied. If the application was approved, a credit card will be received in the mail. The credit card will have an amount that is the approved spending limit. The approved spending limit is the maximum dollar amount that can be owed on the credit card. Each month the credit card company will send an invoice to a mailbox or email.

A Credit Card Statement Will Include:

The Balance Spent

The Payment Due Date

The Minimum Amount Due (can always pay more)

How Much Of The Credit Limit Remains Available To Spend

The Interest Amount In Dollars Charged By The Credit Card Company

The Interest Rate (money charged based on the balance due)

$$ Each month the credit card company will add an interest charge on your account. If your credit card balance is $100 and the interest rate is 10% then an additional $10 will be added to your account. The balance due is now $110. For this reason, it is a good idea to pay off a credit card balance as soon as possible. While a credit card company may only require you to pay $35 from your balance each month, it is helpful to pay more than the minimum balance to be able to get to a zero dollar balance.

Always pay a credit card before the due date. Your credit card payment history is on your credit report and tells others if you pay bills on-time.

Did you know missing a credit card payment will in most situations result in a charge of $25 - $75 added to the amount you owe the company.

Paying credit cards on time will help a company approve a loan in the future. Missing payments will make it very difficult to get a loan from any company or bank.

100 90 80 70 60 50 40 30 20 10 0

The Drawing Board

Review the question and answer shown for number one below. Next, complete questions two and three to compute the time until the balance is paid to $0.

1. A credit card has a balance of $2,000. Interest added to the account is $20 a month. How many months until the balance is paid off if paying $100 a month?

$2,000 balance divided by $100 a month payment = 20 months to pay charges.
There is also $20 a month interest for each of the 20 months.
$20 x 20 months to pay off balance = $400.
How many months would it be to pay the $400 in interest costs?
$400 interest charged divided by $100 a month payment = 4 months.
Total time to pay off the credit card = 24 months.
In ___2___ years and ___0___ months the balance will be paid.

$ $ $

2. A credit card has a balance of $500. Interest added to the account is $20 a month. How many months until the balance is paid off if paying $100 a month?

$_____ balance divided by $____ a month payment = ____ months to pay charges.
There is also $_____ a month interest for each of the _____ months.
Monthly interest $_____X_____ months to pay balance = $_____ interest charged.
How many months would it be to pay the $_____ in interest costs?
$_____ interest charged divided by $_____ a month payment = _____ months.
Total time to pay off the credit card charges and interest costs = _____ months.
In _____ years and _____ months the balance will be paid.

$ $ $

3. A credit card has a balance of $3,000. Interest added to the account is $10 a month. How many months until the balance is paid off if paying $50 a month?

$_____ balance divided by $____ a month payment = ____ months to pay charges.
There is also $_____ a month interest for each of the _____ months.
Monthly interest $_____X_____ months to pay balance = $_____ interest charged.
How many months would it be to pay the $_____ in interest costs?
$_____ interest charged divided by $_____ a month payment = _____ months.
Total time to pay off the credit card charges and interest costs = _____ months.
In _____ years and _____ months the balance will be paid.

$ $ $

APPLY

Your Credit Report

The credit report provides a company considering lending you money with an idea of how reliable you are as a customer. The lending company wants to be sure they are giving their money to a person who is very likely to pay the money back.

- Current & past addresses.
- Open accounts, payment history, credit card limit.
- Current & past names (changes due to marriage/nicknames).
- Closed credit card accounts.

- When the report first began gathering da
- Bankruptcy claims, court judgments, if a
- An overall credit report sco
- A summary of who has requested your credit repo

The credit report may have an error. For this reason, it is suggested that each person view a copy of their credit report to ensure it is accurate. If an error is found the consumer (you) should dispute the item and notify the credit agency to request the correction. The agency will research the information and if confirmed will update your credit report. Credit report mistakes make it difficult to apply for a loan, new credit cards, and even at times applying for a job. A potential employer may review a credit report to confirm that the job candidate has been responsible in their financial decision

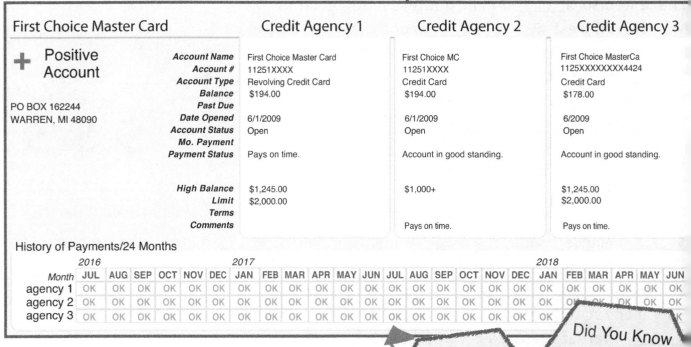

... Sample Credit Report Section .

First Choice Master Card		Credit Agency 1	Credit Agency 2	Credit Agency 3
+ Positive Account	Account Name	First Choice Master Card	First Choice MC	First Choice MasterCa
	Account #	11251XXXX	11251XXXX	1125XXXXXXXX4424
	Account Type	Revolving Credit Card	Credit Card	Credit Card
	Balance	$194.00	$194.00	$178.00
PO BOX 162244	Past Due			
WARREN, MI 48090	Date Opened	6/1/2009	6/1/2009	6/2009
	Account Status	Open	Open	Open
	Mo. Payment			
	Payment Status	Pays on time.	Account in good standing.	Account in good standing.
	High Balance	$1,245.00	$1,000+	$1,245.00
	Limit	$2,000.00		$2,000.00
	Terms			
	Comments		Pays on time.	Pays on time.

History of Payments/24 Months

	2016						2017												2018					
Month	JUL	AUG	SEP	OCT	NOV	DEC	JAN	FEB	MAR	APR	MAY	JUN	JUL	AUG	SEP	OCT	NOV	DEC	JAN	FEB	MAR	APR	MAY	JUN
agency 1	OK	OK	OK	OK	OK	OK	OK	OK	OK	OK	OK	OK	OK	OK	OK	OK	OK	OK	OK	OK	OK	OK	OK	OK
agency 2	OK	OK	OK	OK	OK	OK	OK	OK	OK	OK	OK	OK	OK	OK	OK	OK	OK	OK	OK	OK	OK	OK	OK	OK
agency 3	OK	OK	OK	OK	OK	OK	OK	OK	OK	OK	OK	OK	OK	OK	OK	OK	OK	OK	OK					OK

A credit report gives each person a credit score.

A positive item will result in a higher credit score.

A negative item will result in a lower credit score.

Stay Positive.

OK shows your payment was received on time.

Did You Know
A business has a credit report just like most people have a credit report.

The Drawing Board

Imagine you are preparing to purchase your first home. You know the importance of having an accurate credit report. You request a copy of your most recent credit report to confirm it is correct. Answer the questions below. If the credit report shows the correct information simply mark the item as correct. If the item is not correct mark it as incorrect and write the correct information.

1. In January of 2014 Credit Agency 2 reported your payment as late.

    Correct   Not Correct _____

2. The credit limit on your First Choice Master Card is $4,000.

    Correct   Not Correct _____

3. The credit card number for your First Choice Master Card ends in 6724.

    Correct   Not Correct _____

4. The First Choice Master Card was opened in 2005.

    Correct   Not Correct _____

5. The First Choice Master Card company is located in Dallas, Texas.

    Correct   Not Correct _____

6. The current balance on the First Choice Master Card is $812.

    Correct   Not Correct _____

7. Credit information is shown from four different reporting agencies.

    Correct   Not Correct _____

8. The credit report shows a history of payments received for 36 months.

    Correct   Not Correct _____

9. What are the two credit report mistakes in the section shown?

    _____

INVESTIGATE

Investment Strategy

As you earn money you will begin to consider options for investing.

The investment you select will vary based on several factors including:

How Much Money Am I Investing?   Can I Afford To Lose This Money?

When Do I Need To Withdraw The Money?

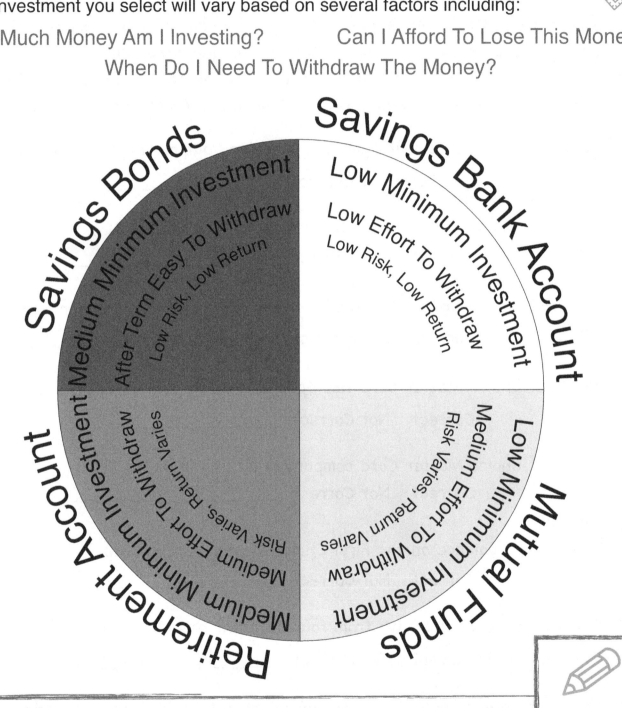

Draw a line to match the term to the definition.

APPLY

1. Withdraw   A. How likely the invested money is to make a profit.

2. Return   B. To take money out of a bank or investment account.

3. Risk   C. The money paid to an investor.

56

The Drawing Board

Consider the following financial questions below. Write your answers in the space provided. Be sure to write the formula used to solve each question.

1. A department store invoice shows the following charges: 1 pair of sneakers $74.95, 1 designer watch by $95.00, 2 pairs of jeans at $50 each. What is the total amount of the invoice?

2. The stock value for Floopy-Doopy Toy Company is $34.25 per share. You have 12 shares of stock. What is the total value of your stock?

3. You are preparing a deposit to bring to the bank for your job at Fluffy Pet Shop. The four checks are written for the following amounts: $20, $41.75, $108.40, $18.12. What is the total amount you of your deposit that you will write on the bank deposit slip?

4. In 2016 your savings account earned $5.25 interest. In 2017 your savings account earned $5.40 interest. In 2018 your account interest total was $5.50. What is the total amount of interest earned?

5. You invested $30 a month for the past 11 months to your 529 college savings account. What was the total amount you invested in your college savings account?

6. The Silly Top Circus is coming to town in five months. A ticket to the show is $50. How much do you need to save each month to purchase a ticket for you and your best friend to see the show?

7. On a rainy day you decided to count the coins in your piggy bank. You empty the piggy bank and divide your coins. You have five quarters, 12 dimes, ten nickels, and 25 pennies. What is the total amount of money in your piggy bank?

THINK

What is A Portfolio?

A portfolio is a summary of investments. Investors are encouraged to invest their money in more than one investment type. Investing in few or more investment types is called diversification. By having a variety of savings, stocks, bonds, and mutual funds an investor can reduce the risk of money loss. If one investment in the portfolio does not return interest or dividends another item in the portfolio may be able to return the money. A **balanced portfolio** is the term used to describe having money in different types of investments.

If an investor has a BALANCED PORTFOLIO they have DIVERSIFIED their investments. Investment DIVERSIFICATION reduces the RISK of losing money.

A diversified portfolio will help reduce loss by seeking to have other investments make up for a loss of money on another investment. A portfolio may be diversified in many different ways. A portfolio of investments with more savings bonds and established company stock has a lower chance of losing the investment money. A portfolio with a high amount of new company stock has a greater risk of losing the financial investment.

Older Age							Young Age
LOW RISK			MEDIUM RISK			HIGH RISK	
conservative							aggressive
Savings Account	Checking Account	Bond	IRA	Mutual Fund	Blue Chip Stock	Stable Corporation Stock	New Corporation Stock

A Piece of Pie

Consider the investment strategy pie charts below. Label each pie chart piece as indicated by writing the percent in the square box provided.

1.

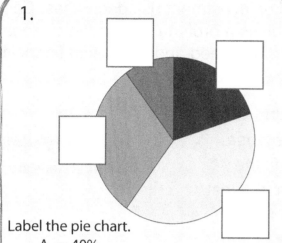

Label the pie chart.
A = 40%
B = 30%
C = 20%
D = 10%

2. Label the pie chart.
Conservative, low risk = 75%
Aggressive, high risk = 25%

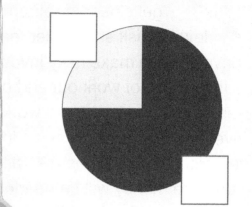

3. What is the dollar value of each section?
A = 25%
B = 25%
C = 50%

The pie chart shows the diversification mix with an investment total value of $12,000.

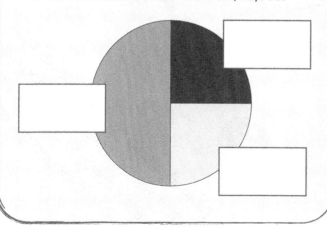

4. An investor has 50% invested in moderate risk stocks. 35% invested in conservative, low-risk stocks and 15% invested in high risk stock.
Label the pie chart to accurately show the pie sections as high, moderate, low.

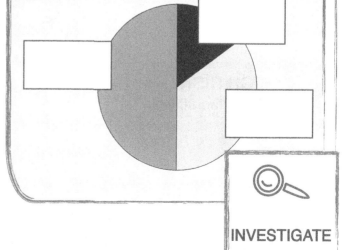

INVESTIGATE

www.YMBAgroup.com

Diversify

Diversifyatopia is an imagined country. A beautiful place where all investment plans are balanced in harmony. Where each investment receives just the right amount of attention. The conditions are so ideal that the overall strategy grows and grows. Citizens of Diversifyatopia choose different levels of risk as the years pass by. As the citizens get closer to retirement the level of investment risk decreases. Each plan gives a profit to reward the citizens for a balanced and diversified financial plan.

As investors get closer to retirement the level of risk should decrease. A young investor can make risky investments because if they do not work out and bring a profit the investor has many years to work to recover the lost investment. However, as an investor is closer to retirement age there is a smaller amount of time until the money will be needed. Therefore, as investors get closer to retirement age the level of risk they are willing to accept will go down. Generally younger investors select more risky investments and older investors select more conservative (less risky) investments. One investment point both will have in common is the need for a diversified portfolio.

NO RISK
Financial Plan 1 year

Age 70

LOW RISK
Financial Plan 5 yrs.

Age 55

MEDIUM RISK
Financial Plan 15 yrs.

Age 40

HIGH RISK
Financial Plan 30 yrs.

Age 25

Diversifyatopia sample financial plan. Each investment plan varies and every investor needs to find the plan to meet their own goals.

The Drawing Board

Congratulations! You have just been promoted to the position of financial advisor at Kash and Pyle Savings Bank. Today you have appointments with six different bank customers who are seeking your suggestions on a custom investment strategy.

Match the bank customer in column one to the investment strategy you would suggest to best match the age, risk level and financial goals of the customer.

Investment Risk Strategy   TOOLBOX

(A) Low Risk   (B) Medium to High Risk   (C) Low to Medium Risk

(D) Medium Risk   (E) High Risk   (F) No Risk to Low Risk

(1) _____ Customer 1 just had their 18th birthday.

(2) _____ Customer 2 is a college student.

(3) _____ Customer 3 just began their first job.

(4) _____ Customer 4 is buying their first house today.

(5) _____ Customer 5 just celebrated 15 years at a job.

(6) _____ Customer 6 is enjoying their retirement.

(7) If you were to invest $100 today which investment risk strategy would you select and why? _____

_____

THINK

This page intentionally left blank.

Y.M.B.A. Finance Review

Congratulations on completing the Y.M.B.A. Finance learning workbook.
Complete the questions below to demonstrate all you have learned.
Write your answers in the spaces provided on page 65.

1. Money an investor earns on a deposit is:

    (A) Stock   (B) Interest   (C) Deposit   (D) Market

2. Company A and Company B join to form Company C. This is a:

    (A) Merger   (B) Sale   (C) Return   (D) Asset

3. Coins and paper money made traveling to trade goods:

    (A) Easier   (B) Faster   (C) More Difficult   (D) Less Common

4. A buckskin was once equal in value to:

    (A) One Bond   (B) One Penny   (C) One Dollar   (D) One Nickel

5. Fiat money is when the value of a currency is based on:

    (A) Sales   (B) Profit   (C) Demand   (D) Gold

6. Until the 1970's in America money issued by the government was backed by:

    (A) Copper and Iron   (B) Land   (C) Diamonds   (D) Gold and Silver

7. The population of people grows at a _____ rate.

    (A) Interest   (B) Unknown   (C) Predictable   (D) Slow

8. _____ guarantees the money will be available for withdrawal at a bank.

    (A) F.D.I.C   (B) E.C.L.N.   (C) H.D.I.O.   (D) N.R.I.T.

9. The person who receives a check and is paid is known as the:

    (A) Payor   (B) Person   (C) Professional   (D) Payee

10. Which of the following is not on the front of a check:

(A) Bank Manager   (B) Date   (C) Memo   (D) Signature

11. When a check is written the check writer enters a record of the payment in a:

(A) Check Register (B) Deposit Slip   (C) Notebook   (D) Binder

12. A check written for an amount greater than the account balance is a:

(A) EJW   (B) CLS   (C) NSF   (D) CMP

13. An account balance adjusted for a deposit or withdrawal is a _____ balance

(A) Growing   (B) Jogging   (C) Running   (D) Adding

14. An unsecured loan is most often a loan between:

(A) Banks   (B) Businesses   (C) Friends   (D) Governments

15. A deposit of $25 is deposited into a savings account. The balance will:

(A) Increase   (B) Decrease   (C) Profit   (D) No Change

16. A negative to using a credit card is the cost of the added:

(A) Interest   (B) Investments   (C) Payroll   (D) Telephone

17. When buying a slice of pizza the most common payment type is:

(A) Loan, Secured (B) Cash   (C) Check   (D) Loan, Unsecured

18. Principal x Rate x Time is the formula used to compute the earned:

(A) Sales   (B) Debt   (C) Expenses   (D) Interest

19. Which of the following is not an ending for a corporate name:

(A) Inc.   (B) Business   (C) Company   (D) Corp.

20. A clearing house is used to transfer _____ between banks.

(A) Customers   (B) Sales   (C) Money   (D) Bonds

1. A separately incorporated company owned by another company is a:

   (A) Department   (B) Division   (C) Subsidiary   (D) Section

2. IPO is the first time a corporation offers _____ for sale.

   (A) Goods   (B) Stock   (C) Products   (D) Services

3. A non-profit corporation does not pay some:

   (A) Taxes   (B) Invoices   (C) Expenses   (D) Bank Fee's

4. The market with the greatest risk of loss of business owner investments is:

   (A) Realism   (B) Communism   (C) Capitalism   (D) Socialism

5. A strategy when buying and selling stocks is to buy _____ and sell _____.

   (A) Low, High   (B) High, Often   (C) Often, Low   (D) High, Low

6. When a shareholder has someone vote for them on their behalf it is a vote by:

   (A) Proxy   (B) Favor   (C) Opinion   (D) Position

7. Par value is the term used for the price of a:

   (A) Bond   (B) Interest Rate   (C) Share of Stock (D) Mutual Fund

8. The stock type that gives the owner voting rights in a corporation is:

   (A) Common   (B) Preferred   (C) Benefit   (D) Demand

9. You have 30 shares of stock in a company that issued a $2 dividend. You earn:

   (A) $6   (B) $50   (C) $60   (D) $65

10. When average stock prices are decreasing over time it is a _____ market.

   (A) Bunny   (B) Buck   (C) Bull   (D) Bear

31. Which item is not printed on the front of a savings bond:

    (A) Maturity Value (B) Date Issued   (C) Owners Name   (D) Interest Rate

32. Which bond type only pays interest on the bond maturity date?

    (A) Asset-Backed (B) Zero Coupon   (C) Floating Rate   (D) Junk Bond

33. A mutual fund benefit is that it joins stocks into a diversified group to reduce:

    (A) Profit   (B) Cost   (C) Risk   (D) Shares

34. An investor can reduce the impact of a stock loss by using:

    (A) Diversification (B) Debt   (C) Demand   (D) Distribution

35. The investment account used to save money for college is a _____ account:

    (A) Checking   (B) 529   (C) 401K   (D) Government

36. An account earns 3% interest a year on a $15,000 balance. Interest earned is:

    (A) $450 per year (B) $150 per year (C) $45 per year   (D) $15 per year

37. Your employer offers a 50% match on your $2,000 401K deposit. Your balance is

    (A) $2,050   (B) $1,000   (C) $3,000   (D) $10,000

38. You own 24 stock shares of the 100 shares issued. What percent do you own?

    (A) 24%   (B) 25%   (C) 76%   (D) 82%

39. Which item is not reported on a personal credit report?

    (A) Library Cards (B) Addresses   (C) Credit Cards   (D) A Credit Score

40. An investor who only purchases stock in new corporations has a _____ strategy

    (A) Low Risk   (B) Balanced   (C) Medium Risk   (D) High Risk

Y.M.B.A. Finance Review Student Test Sheet

Consider the questions on the previous four pages.
Write your answers in the spaces provided below.

1. _____   11. _____   21. _____   31. _____

2. _____   12. _____   22. _____   32. _____

3. _____   13. _____   23. _____   33. _____

4. _____   14. _____   24. _____   34. _____

5. _____   15. _____   25. _____   35. _____

6. _____   16. _____   26. _____   36. _____

7. _____   17. _____   27. _____   37. _____

8. _____   18. _____   28. _____   38. _____

9. _____   19. _____   29. _____   39. _____

10. _____   20. _____   30. _____   40. _____

This page intentionally left blank.

Page 9:

Page 11: (1) ($10x6)+($60x2)+30=60+ 120+30 = $210 (2) ($120 x 2) + $480 = $720 (3) ($60x4) + ($10x8)= $320 (4) $10+$120 = $130 (5) ($30x8) + ($480 2) = $240 + $960 = $1,200 (6) $60 30+$480 = $570

Page 13: graph plots should trend up and increase. (1) 4 million

Page 15: (1) false, more (2) false, money (3) false, Washington, DC (4) false, federal (5) false, does (6) false, money (7) false, law (8) false, closing (9) false, five (10) false, 1920's

Page 17:

Page 18:

ber	Date	Transaction	Withdrawal	√	Deposit	$ 284.00	
3	10/7	Clong Electric September/2014	64	31		219	69
4	10/16	Ace Soccer November/2014	30	50		189	19
	10/20	Babysitting on October 19, 2014			22 00	211	19
5	10/21	TSHS Book Store	25	82		185	37
6	10/24	Dr. Smart	50	00		155	37
	10/25	Gift From Grandma			25 00	160	37
	10/31	Account Interest			1 00	161	37
7	11/7	Dentist Dr. Gold	39	00		122	37
8	11/12	SatTV	30	00		92	37
	11/21	Babysitting on Nov. 21, 2014			40 00	132	37

Page 19:

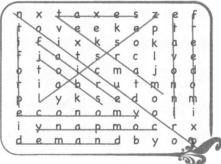

see page 18 check register for 1, 2, 3, register entry. (3) $132.37

Page 21: top to bottom numbers to read: 7, 6, 4, 1, 5, 3, 2.

Page 23: (1) check (2) atm (3) loan secured (4) cash (5) trade (6) loan unsecured (7) credit card (8) electronic payment

Page 25: (2) $2,000x.01 x2 = $40 (3) $4,000x.03x1=$120 (4) $800x.03x3=$72 (5)$40+$120+ $72=$232

Page 27: answers will vary. answers to 1 and 2 should not end in Co., Inc., Incorporated, Company, Corp. or Corporation. Answers 3 and 4 should end in Co., Inc., Incorporated, Corp., Company or Corporation.

Page 29:

cryptogram: competition motivates a business to invent.

Page 31: answers will vary.

Page 33: (1)$21,000 divided by 14,000=$1.50 per share. $1.50 x 1,000 shares = $1,500 (2) $12,600 divided by 3,000 = $4.20 per share. $4.20 x 20 = $84 (3) $30,000 divided by 15,000 =$2.00 per share. $2.00 x 100 = $200 (4) $16,400 divided by 8,000 = $2.05 per share. $2.05 x 400 = $820 (5) $5,250 divided by 3,000=$1.75 per share. $1.75 x 50 = $87.50

Page 35: answers will vary.

Page 37: (1) bull (2) bull (3) bear (4) bear (5) bull (6) bear (7) bear

Page 39: clockwise top left: 4, 3, 8, 9, 7, 10, 6, 2, 5, 1.

Page 41: (1) floating rate (2) junk (3) zero coupon (4) asset backed.

Page 43: answers will vary.

Page 44: answers will vary but should include a benefit of that investment and why the choice was selected.

Page 45: (2) $850 x .04 = $34. $34 + $850 = $884. (3) ($100x12) + ($100 x 12) = $1,200 + $1,200 = $2,400 (4) ($40 x 6) + $500 = $740 (5) ($6,000 x .04)+($2,400 x .04) = $240+$96=$336 $336+$6,000+$2,400=$8,736

Page 47: (1) $200x.02=$4 $200+$4= $204 (2) $25x12=$300 $300x.05= $15 $300+$15=$315 (3) 52-3=49 weeks 49x$2=$98. spent half $98 divided by 2 = $49 saved. (4) $204+$315+$49=$568

Page 49: (1) approved (2) denied (3) approved (4) denied

Page 50: answers will vary but should include a flat tire changed on the road.

Page 51: (1) .5, 50% (2) 1/4, 25% (3) .4, 40% (4) 3/4, .75 (5) 8/10, 80%

Page 53: (2) $500, $100, 5,$20,5,$20,5, $100, $100, $100,$20,5, 5 months plus 5 months = 10 months = 0 years 10 months. (3) $3,000,$50,60,$10,60,$10,60,$600, $600,$600,$50,12,60 months +12 months = 72 months = 6 years, zero months.

Page 55: all not correct. (1) never late (2) $2,000 (3) agency 3, 4424 (4) 2009 (5) Warren, MI (6) $178 (7) 3 (8) 24 months (9) card balance on agency 1, listed as auto loan by agency 2.

Page 56: (1) B (2) C (3) A

Page 57: (1) $74.95+$95+$50+$50= $269.95 (2) $34.25x12=$411 (3) $20+ $41.75+$108.40+$18.12=$187.77 (4) $5.25+$5.40+$5.50=$16.15 (5)$30x11= $330 (6) $50x2=$100 then $100 divided by 5 months = $20 a month to save. (7) (.25x5)+(.10x12)+(.05x10)+(.01x25)=$3.20

Page 59:

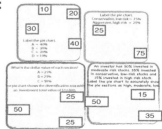

Page 61: (1) E (2) B (3) D (4) C (5) A (6) F (7) Answers will vary.

   www.YMBAgroup.com

Y.M.B.A. Finance Review Answer Key

1. B	11. A	21. C	31. D
2. A	12. C	22. B	32. B
3. A	13. C	23. A	33. C
4. C	14. C	24. C	34. A
5. C	15. A	25. A	35. B
6. D	16. A	26. A	36. A
7. C	17. B	27. C	37. C
8. A	18. D	28. A	38. A
9. D	19. B	29. C	39. A
10. B	20. C	30. D	40. D

www.YMBAgroup.com

Certificate of Completion

Presented To

_____

Upon Successful Completion

of the

Youth Master of Business Administration

FINANCE

_____
Presented By

_____
Date

Thank you for learning with Y.M.B.A. workbooks.

Y.M.B.A.
Single
Topic
Learning
Workboks

Lesson Pages,
Worksheets,
A Quiz
and
A Certificate

Learn
Life Skills
&
Business
with
Y.M.B.A.

Benefit from 100 top tips and tricks that will enhance the effectiveness and enjoyment of your Internet-based virtual classroom presented by virtual teacher, recruiter and trainer, L.J. Keller. A must-have book for anyone considering, or currently teaching, English virtually as a second language! Benefit from ideas, techniques and examples for English lanugage learners. These easy to implement concepts can enhance your classroom and effectively increase your students comprehension. Students also enjoy learning in this active learner classroom environment. Ideas are presented with clarity using examples that can provide you with a competitive advantage in the virtual classroom. Enjoy this all-in-one solution to help you launch and sustain amazing student results. **Are you ready to be an amazing virtual teacher?**

Do you know someone who would like to work from home? Virtual teaching is a wonderful option! Work from home. Flexible schedules. Amazing students!

Ready to define your S.P.A.C.E.?
Do you know your 4 E's?

www.YMBAgroup.com

ISBN 9781690614036

This one book can help you quickly achieve a successful virtual classroom.

100 Tips are ready to assist!

Recruiting for virtual teachers with a four year college degree, any major at:
www.YMBAgroup.com

100 Virtual ESL Teacher Tips and Tricks

Proven Ideas For Student Enjoyment and Success!

L.J. Keller, M.B.A.

SPLASH: A waterpark mystery

Moore Mysteries | Book 1

The champion is part of a secret plan! Solve the mystery as you meet Battle, twins Rachel and Reese, Zack and Morgan as they travel the United States with their parents. In this first book in the series the family begin a road trip adventure. The first family fun stop finds a mystery the family works together to solve. Join the family as they race to tell the judges to plan they discovered. What was the secret plan? Will the kids find the judges in time?

GRADES 2-4/AGES 6-8/EARLY CHAPTER BOOK

Look Inside!

Skill Builder practice and a Book Quiz Included

Engaging Reading Books plus
Skill Builders & a Book Quiz
An easy way to demonstrate
learning accomplishments.

Chapter Books That Are Fun To Read and Include A Quiz To Demonstrate Completion

57 Days
Miriam Short Sails with William Penn

57 Days Miriam Short Sails With William Penn

Learning Book Quiz Included!

YMBA Days In History Series

Join Miriam, Adam and Anne Mary, on their journey from England to America with William Penn to see the land he was granted in the New World by the King of England. Exciting history based on actual people and events. Experience the triumphs, struggles, loss and dreams while traveling across the Atlantic Ocean to a new home. Discover the path so many experienced as they left their home for America. Details vividly paint a picture of the conditions on the ship and the difficult days along the way. What challenges did they endure? What were the fears and hopes of the young adults? An exciting historical adventure of the journey to America. Join Miriam on her voyage with her family and William Penn.

GRADES 6-10/AGES 11-15/ FACTION CHAPTER BOOK

Made in United States
Orlando, FL
17 August 2024

50393177R00043